KYOTO

京都 & 奈良

NARA

✦

The Soul of Japan

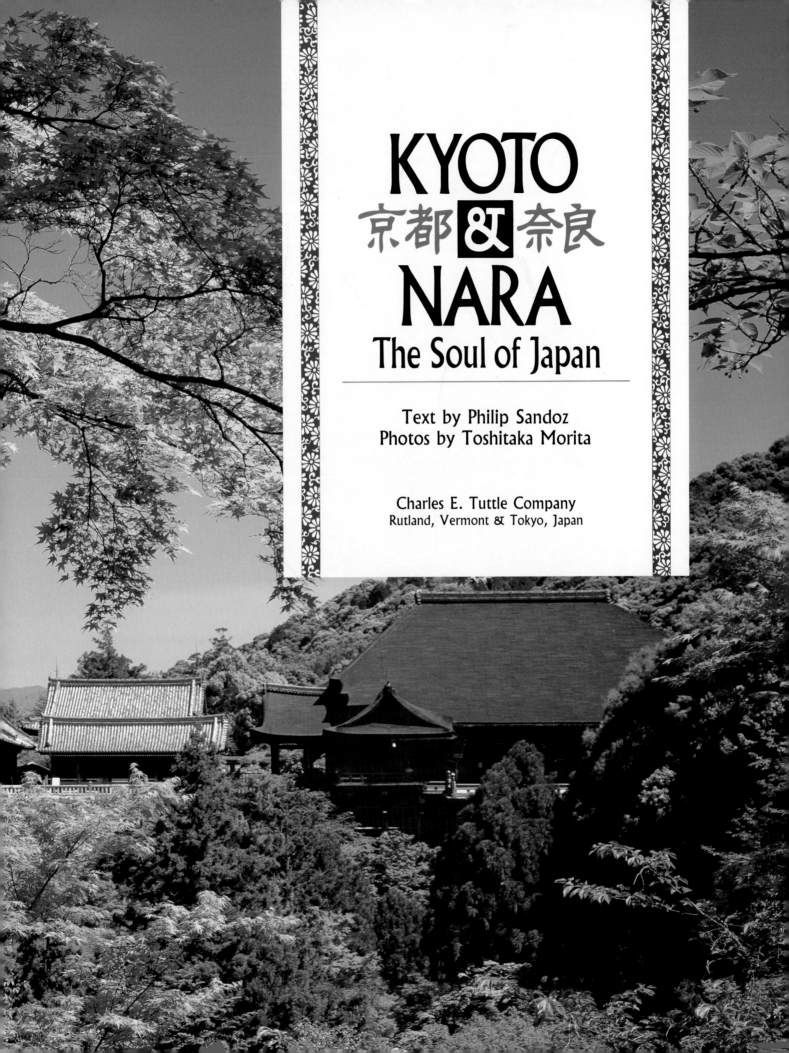

KYOTO
京都 & 奈良
NARA
The Soul of Japan

Text by Philip Sandoz
Photos by Toshitaka Morita

Charles E. Tuttle Company
Rutland, Vermont & Tokyo, Japan

(Pages 2–3): *Autumn scene at Tanzan Shrine.*
(Pages 4–5): *Yakushi-ji in the light of dawn.*
(Title page): *Spring greenery surrounds Kiyomizu-dera.*

Note: To avoid redundancy, the suffixes *-ji* and *-dera* (temple) are used appropriately herein and their translation remains omitted.

Map illustrations by Shigeko Nakayama

Published by the Charles E. Tuttle Company, Inc.
of Rutland, Vermont and Tokyo, Japan
with editorial offices at
2-6 Suido 1-chome, Bunkyo-ku, Tokyo 112

© 1994 by Charles E. Tuttle Publishing Co., Inc.

LCC Card No. 93-60523
ISBN 0-8048-1916-5

First edition, 1994

Printed in Singapore

Contents

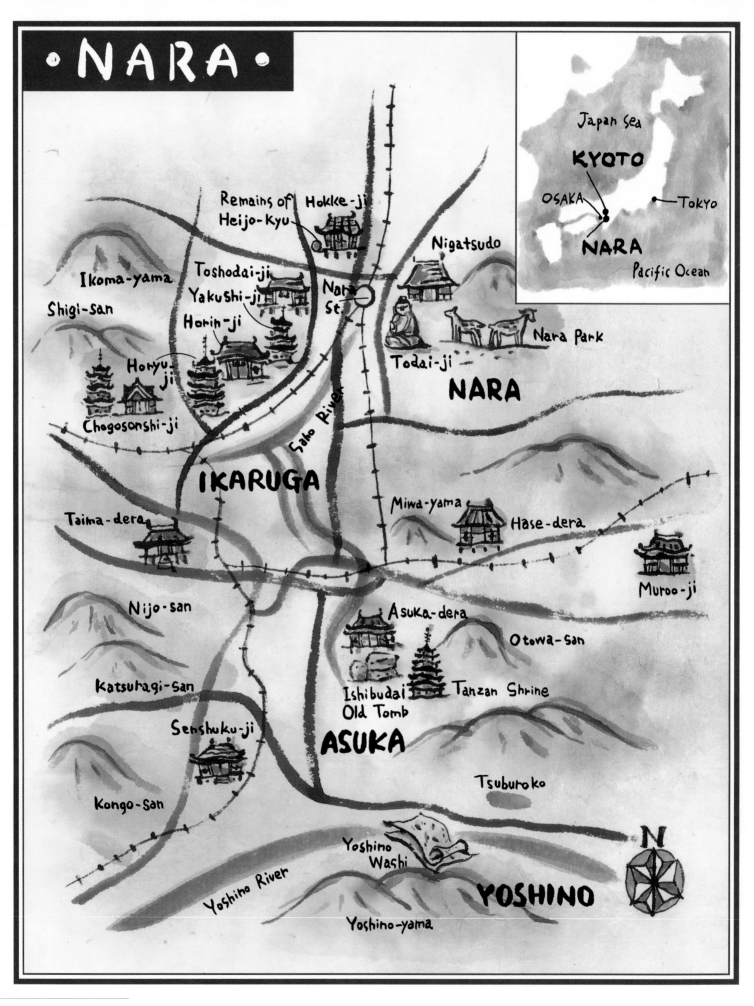

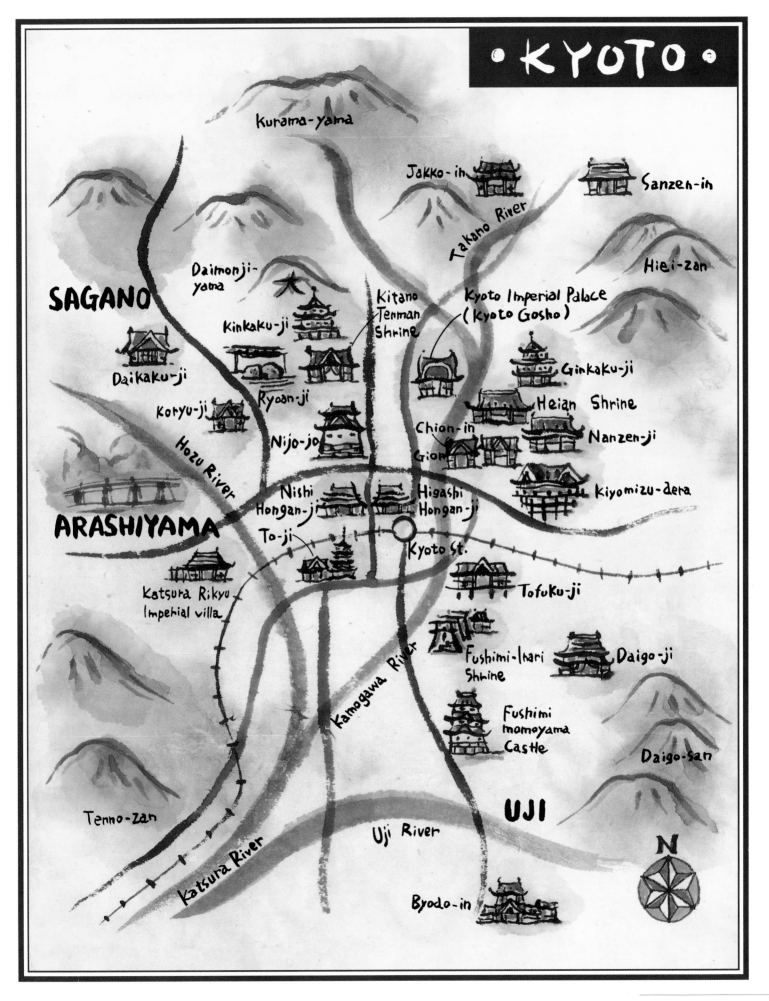

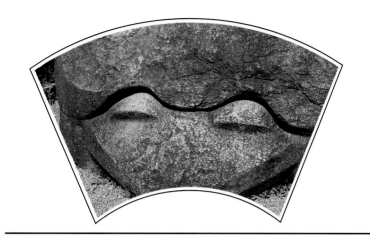

Introduction

Visitors to modern-day Japan tend to be either impressed or depressed, depending on their viewpoints and expectations. Arriving at an international airport in Japan is no different from arriving, say, in London, Lisbon, or Los Angeles. The Hyatts, Hiltons, and Holiday Inns could be in Miami, Manchester, or Melbourne. Walks along the main streets of Tokyo or Osaka or almost any other Japanese city turn up little different from any Western city. The eyes are filled with tall buildings, designer-brand shops, and well-dressed people; and the ears are assaulted by traffic noise, loudspeakers, and the normal cacophony of urban life anywhere in the world. All in all, those arriving in Japan expecting Zen-like tranquillity and inklings of an ancient culture could well be disappointed.

This need not be so. Stray just a little from the paved boulevards and traditional Japan rapidly reasserts itself. Narrow alleys, wooden houses, small temples and tiny shrines, statues of the major gods, goddesses, and thousands of minor deities, public bathhouses, mom and pop stores, beautifully manicured gardens the size of tea trays, paper lanterns, paper doors, paper street decorations, the call of street vendors, the gush of laughter, the scream of school children, and the shrill of insects all contribute to what Japan has always been, and what it remains today.

It is often claimed, usually by the Japanese themselves, that Japanese culture is unique. In a way this is true, but not for the reasons often given. Japanese people, Japanese culture, even Japanese religion have not descended in unbroken lines from the actions and ideas of pure Japanese gods, goddesses, and gurus. The rich blend of cultures that comprises the Japan of today is different from that of any other country, but in actuality is the hybrid result of thousands of years of in-

fluences, initially from the early civilizations of China, India, and Asia in general, and later from Europe and the United States. Differences from the originals are myriad, as all cultural imports to Japan have faced century upon century of adaptation, refinement, and Japanization.

Even Japan's imperial system, the longest unbroken line of sovereigns anywhere in the world, owes much to ideas borrowed from other Asian courts and countries and then adapted to the needs of Japanese people and society.

Visits to the country's two most ancient extant capitals, Nara and Kyoto, reinforce this sense of Asianness, but also strengthen understanding of the variety and depth of the culture that can be said to be unique to Japan. Animistic Shinto shrines abut Buddhist temples, imperial residences are surrounded by warrens of artisan dwellings, aspects of Japan's violent and militaristic past lie cheek and jowl with memories of great poets and scholars. All of these, however, are not merely museum pieces, but are distinct, almost breathing descendants of the Japan of yesterday. No understanding of modern Japan is possible without at least a cursory knowledge of what Japan was and where its customs and mores come from.

Prior to the founding of Nara (Heijokyo)

in 710, Japan did not have a permanent capital city, and it was during the Nara period (646–794) that Japan experienced its first genuine flowering of indigenous culture. Even so, Nara, as was Kyoto later, was chosen because its situation met the requirements of Chinese geomancy, and was laid out according to the precepts of Chinese T'ang dynasty town planning. The selection of the site was also probably influenced by the proximity of several important Buddhist temples, such as Horyu-ji, founded in 607.

During the seventy-four years that Nara remained the capital, the strength of Buddhism, not only religiously but politically, grew rapidly and, in fact, it was the overwhelming strength of the monasteries that decided the imperial government to move the capital to Kyoto (Heiankyo) in 794, where it remained until 1868. The Heian period (794–1185) brought centuries of relative peace and prosperity to Japan and can be said to be the true source of Japanese culture as we understand it today.

Both Nara and Kyoto helped define Japan and the Japanese and there is still a great deal to see and experience within both cities that would undoubtedly help today's visitor learn to understand where modern Japan came from and, ultimately, where it is heading.

Ancient stone relics from early civilizations can still be seen in several areas around Nara and Kyoto.

RIGHT: *Sakafune Stone at Asuka village in Nara.*
BELOW: *The Ishibutai Tomb, thought to be that of Soga no Umako, dates from the seventh century.*

Tranquillity is undiluted in and around Nara.

LEFT: *The morning mist shrouds Miwayama before the heat of the day brings a sharpness to the scene.*

BELOW: *Lotus leaves spread serenely over the surface of a pond in the recently excavated remains of Nara's Heijo Palace site.*

Religion, both native and imported, played an important role in the establishment and growth of both Nara and Kyoto.

LEFT: *The Great Buddha in Todai-ji.*
RIGHT: *Stone image of Amanojaku, a supernatural creature often described in folk tales, at Takagamo Shrine.*
BELOW: *Stone monkey figures at the Kibihime-no-miko burial site in Asuka village.*

ABOVE: *Part of the two-and-a-half-mile-long avenue of torii presented over the years by worshippers at Fushimi-Inari Shrine in Kyoto.*

LEFT: *A selection of Buddhist statues stands guard at Kamidaigo-ji, Kyoto.*

An imperial-style barge traverses Osawano Pond against a striking backdrop of autumn leaves.

Imperial Nara

Japanese imperial history can be said to have started in 660 B.C., when Emperor Jimmu was enthroned in the town of Kashiwabara, near today's Osaka, after battling his way from the southern island of Kyushu to the area now regarded as the cradle of Japanese culture. During these battles, the first emperor came up against many ferocious tribes, then called *emishi,* a word meaning barbarian, who are thought to be the ancestors of the Ainu, a people eventually banished from mainstream Japanese culture but who still survive in isolated areas in Japan's northern island of Hokkaido.

Japan's imperial heritage, therefore, has existed, at least according to legend, in an unbroken line for over twenty-five centuries. However, for the thirteen hundred years beginning with the enthronement of Jimmu, the country never had a permanent capital city, due to an ancient belief that a place was polluted by death, making it necessary to relocate the capital each time an emperor died.

This belief, though considerably watered down by the centuries, was still evident on the death of Emperor Showa (Hirohito) in 1989. His son, Emperor Heisei (Akihito), upon enthronement, was not allowed to move into the existing Imperial Palace in Tokyo, but had to wait until a new residence was built for him, albeit within the same compound.

The modern approach to the siting of the imperial residence can be dated back to the year 710, when Empress Gemmyo moved the capital to Heijokyo, present-day Nara, where it remained for the next seventy-four years. It is not recorded exactly why Nara was chosen, but no doubt the strong relations with the T'ang dynasty of China and the influence of Chinese geomancy, *fengshui,*

with its reliance on the spiritual correctness of air and water, were important factors.

Also of vital importance would have been the proximity to several leading Buddhist establishments including Horyu-ji, founded in 607, and Yakushi-ji, founded in 680, both of which helped establish Nara as the heart of Japanese Buddhism.

The city itself owes much to the early Chinese influences, being laid out according to Chinese town-planning principles on a rectangular grid modeled on the layout of Ch'ang-an (today's Xian), then the capital city of China.

During the Nara period, Japan officially adopted the Buddhist religion, was strongly influenced by Chinese art, and retained close connections with China, with official embassies being exchanged. The Chinese influence reached its peak during the rule of Emperor Shomu, who promoted Buddhism by imperial decree, commissioned the Great Buddha *Daibutsu,* a fifty-foot-high bronze statue of the Buddha, and provided for the construction of provincial temples throughout the country.

The height to which Buddhist culture rose during the Nara period is, perhaps, best seen at Todai-ji, one of the most beautiful examples of the temple architecture of the period. The Hall of the Great Buddha *Daibutsuden* was reconstructed in 1708, and though smaller than the original building, is still the largest wooden structure in the world. Also in Todai-ji, just east of the *Daibutsuden,* stands an old bell tower containing the second largest bell in Japan (nine feet high and thirteen feet in diameter), originally cast in 749. Throughout the Nara period, Buddhism seemed all-powerful.

Ironically, it was the strength of Buddhism, particularly as it came to militarily and politically challenge the power of the government, that led to the decision to move the capital a few miles to Nagaoka in 784.

Despite having been abandoned as the home of government over twelve hundred years ago, Nara retains the atmosphere of an ancient capital, having practically no industry, but a wealth of religious and cultural sites to fascinate today's visitors. After the capital was moved to Kyoto, the city spread eastwards. The historic center of Nara now lies on its outskirts and has, consequently, escaped the destruction of modernization and Westernization.

RIGHT: *This bell, typical of the style used in temples throughout Japan, has no clapper and is tolled by being struck on the outside with a log. The notes are long, deep, and sonorous.*

BELOW: *The Zen garden at Hokke-ji provides a perfect sense of simplicity and tranquillity.*

Nara's climate is temperate, but the seasons do bring dramatic changes of color.

OVERLEAF: *Yakushi-ji surrounded by the fresh colors of spring.*
RIGHT: *Flowering cherry trees mantel Ono-dera.*
BELOW: *The lushness of summer, as shown by the rich greens of the irises at Hokke-ji.*

The five-story pagoda at Hase-dera is almost hidden by the thriving foliage of spring.

ABOVE: *The Nigatsu-do of Todai-ji, which was founded in 745 at the request of Emperor Shomu, a devout Buddhist.*

LEFT: *Weathered timbers, such as those at Oka-dera, add a sense of graceful antiquity to many Nara buildings.*

RIGHT: *A cluster of Buddhist icons at Kofuku-ji, originally erected in Kyoto in 678 but transferred to its present site in 710.*

BELOW: *The eighteen-foot-high Senju Kannon (One-Thousand-Arm Kannon) at Toshodai-ji.*

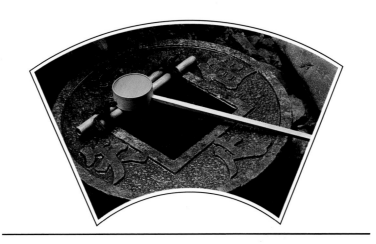

Imperial Kyoto

During the Nara period, as described earlier, Buddhist monasteries and the monks themselves increasingly became serious players in politics, with the result that by 784 the emperor decided that close proximity to such institutions was a threat to imperial power. Nagaoka, a village some thirty miles from Nara, was the site originally chosen to house the capital. Its ascendancy, however, was short-lived. Ten years later, after several misfortunes had rocked the imperial family, Nagaoka came to be thought of as a place of evil spirits and the capital was moved yet again. The site chosen was the village of Uda, which was renamed Heiankyo (capital of peace), later also known as Miyako (imperial residence), and eventually, after the Meiji Restoration of the nineteenth century, Kyoto (capital city).

During the almost eleven hundred years Kyoto remained the capital of Japan many changes occurred. The country developed from a collection of fiefdoms into the initial stages of democratic power. In 794, however, the Chinese influence over Japan was still very strong, and, as Nara had been, Kyoto was planned along Chinese lines as a walled city with a double moat. Shortly after the move to Kyoto, political power was removed from the imperial family with the country being in effect run by a series of clans and ultimately by a succession of powerful shoguns. This resulted in the flowering of Kyoto as the artistic and religious center it remains today.

Almost every aspect of what we now consider Japanese culture and civilization was nurtured during Kyoto's period as capital. The artistic range and religious depth of the city and its surrounds are awe-inspiring, ranging from perhaps the greatest collection of ancient Japanese art and artifacts to some of

the most magnificent temples and shrines anywhere in the country.

The wealth of Kyoto is perhaps best expressed by Ginkaku-ji (Silver Temple) and Kinkaku-ji (Golden Temple), both originally built in the late fourteenth century as private residences for Ashikaga Yoshimitsu, the third shogun of the Muromachi *bakufu* (military government). Kinkaku-ji is particularly spectacular, representing three distinct architectural styles: Heian period (first floor), Kamakura period (second floor), and Chinese *karayo* (third floor), all gilded and reflected in a neighboring lake.

The religious aspects of Kyoto and its characteristic tranquillity are typified by the many gardens throughout the city, ranging from the iris gardens at Heian Shrine to the cherry blossoms at Daigo-ji or the Zen rock garden at Nanzen-ji. One of the earliest temples to be built after Kyoto became the capital was Kiyomizu-dera (798), which offers a breathtaking view over the city from a wooden verandah that seems magically to hang in midair over precipitous wooded hillsides. The verandah appears to ignore the law of gravity, and its construction gave birth to the Japanese phrase which means to participate in any dangerous act, but literally translates "to jump from the Kiyomizu-dera verandah."

Kyoto's imperial history may best be represented by Nijo Castle, originally built by the shogun Tokugawa Ieyasu in 1603, but the site from where Emperor Meiji issued an edict abolishing the shogunate in 1868, heralding Japan's emergence as a budding Western-style democracy and sounding the death knell of isolationism and feudalism.

Almost everywhere one turns in Kyoto, history is tangibly present. What shouldn't be forgotten, however, is how the city came to be chosen as the capital of Japan. As mentioned before, the ancient Japanese superstitions about the siting of a city, particularly an imperial city, could only be assuaged by the careful following of the strictures of geomancy, what the Chinese call *fengshui*, wherein the quality of the surrounding air is taken into account and balanced with the auspicious configuration of nearby hills and streams. This careful siting resulted not only in Kyoto remaining the capital for over one thousand years, but in the beautiful and peaceful surroundings that the city enjoys even now at the end of the twentieth century.

LEFT: *This massive paper lantern at Gyogan-ji is typical of those seen in temples throughout Japan. The rope hanging behind the lantern is pulled to ring a bell when prayers are offered.*

BELOW: *The verandah at Kiyomizu-dera provides one of the most breathtaking views of Kyoto.*

The corner tower of Nijo Castle sits on a solid foundation of carefully cut stones.

Gardens and ponds abound throughout Kyoto and are a constant source of relaxation.

LEFT: *The Zen garden at Gokonomiya Shrine.*
BELOW LEFT and RIGHT: *Azaleas bloom in full glory in springtime, while autumn is heralded by a carpet of crimson leaves.*

ABOVE: *Ginkaku-ji (Silver Temple) nestles among trees at the edge of a still and ancient pond.*

RIGHT: *The magnificent iris garden at Heian Shrine gives the impression of nature run majestically riot.*

LEFT: *A traditional cherry-blossom scene at the five-story pagoda of Daigo-ji.*

BELOW: *A walk in the hills outside Kyoto can be deliciously and peacefully broken with a stop at an elegant tea shop.*

RIGHT: *The wooden architecture of the bell towers in many temples, such as this one at Mimurodo-ji, provides a cooling aspect, even on a hot summer's day.*

BELOW: *Nanzen-ji garden, perhaps the most famous example of Zen garden design.*

Timeless Nara

Even a short visit to Nara proves why the city and its surrounds are usually referred to as the cradle of Japanese culture. There are few cities in the world that exhibit such a sense of timelessness and spirituality. Over seven hundred years before Christopher Columbus discovered America, Nara, a city with a population of over two hundred thousand, was the political capital and cultural heart of a growing empire.

The pure antiquity of the area is perhaps best understood through a visit to Horyu-ji, the oldest original temple complex in Japan and a marvelous example of Asuka-period (552–646) architecture. It is believed to have originated in 586, when Japan's first Buddhist emperor, Yomei Tenno, was stricken with a serious illness and decreed that a statue of Yakushi-Nyorai, the Healing Buddha, be built. Unfortunately, the decree was too late and he died before completion of the statue.

Though not efficacious for that emperor, the belief in the healing powers of Buddhist statuary continued, and can be experienced to this day at Todai-ji, where a statue of Binzuru is said to cure any illness if touched by one hand while the other hand is held over the ailing part of the body.

Whether a visit to Nara can actually help the physically ill is debatable, but certainly a trip to the city is the perfect antidote to the stress of modern living. Nara lies surrounded by woods, fertile farmland, and mountains providing breathtaking panoramas of the city. Although packed with a wealth of ancient building and religious sites, Nara still manages to retain the atmosphere of a bucolic small town.

The peacefulness of the city is obvious almost immediately one steps off the train. Within a few minutes the visitor can be whisked into the past by a walk through Nara

(Page 42): *The East Pagoda at Yakushi-ji.*

Park, at thirteen hundred acres the largest of its kind in Japan. Contained within its confines are many ancient buildings and tranquil areas of centuries-old woodland inhabited by hundreds of partly tame roe deer. No visit to the park is complete without a view of the five-story pagoda of Kofuku-ji stunningly reflected in the waters of Sarusawano Pond.

Buddhism is omnipresent throughout Nara and its environs, and there is probably nowhere else in Japan with such a treasury of the oldest, the biggest, or the most powerful Buddhist buildings, statuary, and art.

One of the "Seven Great Temples of Nara" that should certainly not be missed is Todai-ji, the head temple of Kegon Buddhism, a sect founded in 736 by a Chinese priest and teaching the attractive theology that every person is capable of attaining enlightenment.

Within the precincts of Todai-ji is the Great Buddha *Daibutsu,* a tribute to early Japanese casting. It stands 53 feet high, was cast from 437 tons of bronze, 286 pounds of gold, and 7 tons of wax, and is the largest such statue in Japan. Behind the Great Buddha are statues of two celestial guardians, Komokuten and Tamonten. Just in front of Tamonten is a gigantic wooden column containing a hole near the ground. Many people believe that if a person can crawl through the hole, he or she is guaranteed a place in heaven. It may be worth trying.

Paradoxically, in contrast to many of its great buildings the city of Nara itself is surprisingly small, and can easily be visited in a single day, but if time permits, the traveler should keep an extra day for trips to the areas lying outside the city precincts, all easily reachable by public transport. Of particular interest is Yakushi-ji, another of the "Seven Great Temples of Nara," founded in 680, thirty years before the city became Japan's capital. This temple contains many great buildings and treasures, including the over thirteen-hundred-year-old East Pagoda, the only surviving building of the Hakuho period of Buddhist architecture.

Few visitors to Nara will be disappointed by the ancient city. Through a study of the city's buildings, relics, and art, will come a deeper understanding of both the origins of Japan and how Japanese culture, religion, and mores developed.

RIGHT: *The five-story pagoda at Kofuku-ji in Nara Park as seen through a halo of cherry blossoms.*

BELOW: *The partly tame roe deer in Nara Park have become one of the city's most popular tourist attractions.*

ABOVE: *Chogosonshi-ji on Mount Shigi blends perfectly with its natural surroundings.*

RIGHT: *A fine sprinkling of snow adds a touch of austere beauty to the entrance of Hasedera.*

(Pages 46–47): *Sunset as seen from the verandah of Nigatsu-do, Todai-ji.*

ABOVE: *The five-story pagoda at Kofuku-ji stands behind the weeping willows surrounding Sarusawano Pond.*

RIGHT: *A traditional, free-standing bell tower of Chinese-inspired architectural design at Todai-ji.*

LEFT: *A five-story pagoda is surrounded by the trees at Muroo-ji.*

BELOW: *The stairway to Muroo-ji is garlanded by the final fiery glory of autumn.*

ABOVE: *Whatever the weather, Japanese landscaping and architecture always harmonizes with nature.*

LEFT: *Less famous than the cherry blossoms but just as beautiful, persimmon trees frame Horin-ji.*

51

Arts and crafts flourish in and around Nara.

ABOVE LEFT: *Traditional chopsticks.*
ABOVE RIGHT: *The making of Yoshino paper.*
LEFT: *The intricate design of a waxed-paper umbrella.*

RIGHT: *Japanese noodles hanging out to dry.*

BELOW: *Bags made from and decorated with Japanese paper.*

Timeless Kyoto

To people of many countries, a century may seem a very, very long time. In 1895, for instance, the unified country of Germany was less than fifteen years old, Italy had been formed thirty-five years previously, and in the United States President Grover S. Cleveland was busy cutting a swath through the civil service, upsetting the wealthy and dishonest. In Kyoto in 1895, a new shrine was built. In a city of shrines and temples this may not seem particularly significant, but Heian Shrine was built to commemorate the eleven hundredth anniversary of the founding of the city. Kyoto had become the capital city of Japan in 794, when the barbarian Germanic tribes were picking the carcass of the Roman Empire, and the Mayas were the nearest civilization to Washington.

The continuity of culture, religion, and the arts that Kyoto nurtured for well over a thousand years is typified by Kiyomizu-dera, founded in 798, a mere four years after the city became the capital. The strength of Buddhism in the Japan of that time may seem to have been overwhelming, but even though Kiyomizu-dera is dedicated to the Eleven-Headed Kannon, an import, the Japanese were already showing a great ability to assimilate and Japanize. For example, in the entrance to the hall that houses the Buddhist Kannon are two sandals cast of iron that are said to have been worn by a giant slain by Issun-boshi, a cross between Tom Thumb and Jack the Giant Killer in Japanese folklore. Giants there may be no longer, but the architectural magnificence of the temple and its eyrie-like setting certainly make it possible to believe in their prior existence.

The surrounding hills and mountains afford visitors to Kyoto many spectacular views of the entire city, from the modern, concrete central areas to the still traditional area of

(Page 54): *The haunting elegance of Momoyama Castle.*

Gion, an entertainment district of narrow alleys crammed with tea houses, theaters, craft shops, and excellent but expensive restaurants. A walk through these streets will transport the tourist hundreds of years back into the past, as the busy stores will remind him of Japan's centuries-old mercantile tradition.

The owners of Gion businesses, as well as many other merchants and tradesmen from throughout the city, make their way annually to Fushimi-Inari Shrine, dedicated to the goddess of rice-growing, but now believed to bring prosperity to all business concerns. The strength of this belief is demonstrated by the two-and-a-half-mile avenue leading up to the shrine, spanned almost continuously by hundreds of red torii presented to the shrine by worshippers.

Although some shrines and temples seem to have been taken over by materialistic worshippers, there is still much of Kyoto that reflects the more traditional Japanese ethics of peace and tranquillity. A perfect example of such beliefs can be found in the Zen garden at Ryoan-ji, a totally stylized display of rocks and raked white sand.

There is so much to see in Kyoto that the visitor may easily be convinced to stay reasonably close to the center of the city and take one of the organized tours. This, though enjoyable, would be a mistake. Twelve hundred years has allowed the surrounding areas of Kyoto time to develop and to avoid the constant modernization, some say desecration, of the city itself by generation upon generation of city planners and other philistines. One short side trip that is worthwhile is to Byodo-in, a temple built on the site of the former country residence of a warlord. Byodo-in contains many eleventh-century works of art and is itself one of the finest remaining examples of Heian-period architecture.

Tourists should try to avoid visiting Kyoto in the main summer season, which is usually extremely hot and humid as well as ridiculously crowded. Springtime in Kyoto is marvelous and, during that season, visitors can experience the deep greens of rice and tea fields, as well as the lush silence of nearby mountains and the spiritual cleanliness of waterfalls and rushing streams. Autumn, when the wooded hillsides appear on fire with the dramatic fall foliage, is also extravagantly beautiful.

As Kyoto attracts over ten million visitors a year, it is best to carefully plan a trip that does not include weekends or national holidays, but under no circumstances should the traveler in Japan not experience one of the country's most beautiful treasuries of culture, religion, and art.

RIGHT: *Teradaya, a traditional Japanese inn of the style still found in some of the older areas of Kyoto.*

BELOW: *Matsuo-ji, a striking example of the less famous but equally beautiful temples of Kyoto and its surrounding area.*

The abundance of pure water was one of the reasons Kyoto was selected as the capital.

LEFT: *A boat carries barrels of saké through the city.*
BELOW: *The Keiryu Bridge over the Biwako-sosui Canal as seen through its background of cherry blossoms.*

ABOVE: *A pure stream burbles through a cedar forest in Kitayama on a winter's morning.*

LEFT: *A traditional boat is punted under the autumn leaves in Arashiyama.*

LEFT: *Byodo-in sits serenely, as if on its own desert island.*

BELOW: *The three-story pagoda at Kiyomizu-dera floats above a sea of cherry blossoms.*

RIGHT: *Kitano Tenman Shrine seems to hover over a lake of sand.*

BELOW: *Kinkaku-ji (Golden Temple) surrounded by a storm of snow.*

The colors and tones of Kyoto bedazzle the eyes and tantalize the mind.

ABOVE: *The lush green of a tea field with bushes arranged in steps down a hillside.*
LEFT: *Spring brings myriad hues to the Rakusui garden at Jonan Shrine.*

LEFT: *Camellias add magic to the stone stair-way at Honen-in.*

BELOW: *Autumn tints and deep red textiles herald the oncoming winter at Hiranoya in Okusagano.*

ABOVE: *Cool green moss covers the ground at Sanzen-in.*

LEFT: *The rebirth of the year is accompanied by brilliant, fresh green growth along the entryway to Sanzen-in.*

The Japanese sense of serenity is a combination of simplicity and naturalness.

RIGHT: *A bamboo ladle waits to refresh the traveller with pure water from a well in the Rakusui garden.*

BELOW: *Islands of rocks amid a sea of sand bring a peaceful prospect to the Zen garden at Ryoan-ji.*

Traditional Festivals

Tourists to Kyoto and Nara will not only be able to visit many of the most magnificent temples and shrines in Japan and view many priceless works of religious art, but should also be able to experience at least one of the festivals, many of which date back a thousand years or more. The listing below is not complete, as such a catalogue would require a book of its own, but the festivals and events selected are many of the most visually pleasing and religiously important to be experienced in Japan.

Dates of festivals vary slightly from year to year, so visitors are strongly advised to check the exact dates with a travel agency. Festivals and events are listed here by date, Japanese title when possible, English explanation, and location.

KYOTO FESTIVALS

January 1 *Okera-mairi,* believers light torches from the sacred flame with which they cook the first meal of the year, Yasaka Shrine.

Early January *Kemari-hajime,* the playing of a traditional ball game, Shimogamo Shrine.

Early January *Toka Ebisu,* festival in honor of Ebisu, the god of fortune, Ebisu Shrine.

Mid-January *Ho Onkyo,* festival in memory of Shinran, the founder of the Jodo Shinshu sect, Nishi Hongan-ji.

Mid-January *Hadaka Odori,* dance by nearly naked men, Hokai-ji.

Mid-January *Toshiya,* traditional archery contest, Sanjusangen-do.

Late January temple festival in memory of Kobo Daishi, founder of the Shingon sect, To-ji.

Early February *Setsubun,* bean-throwing ceremony, many temples and shrines.

Late February *Baikasai,* open-air tea ceremony under plum blossoms, Kitano Tenman Shrine.

Early March *Hina Matsuri,* doll festival, Hokyo-ji.

Mid-March *Nehan-e,* memorial of Buddha's death, several temples.

Early April *Hana Matsuri,* Buddha's birthday, all temples.

Second Sunday in April *Taiko-no-Hanami Gyoretsu,* procession in traditional clothes under cherry blossoms, Daigo-ji.

Second Sunday in April *Yasurai Matsuri,* warding-off-of-demons dance, Imamiya Ebisu Shrine.

Mid-April *Jusan-mairi,* festival for thirteen-year-old children, Horin-ji.

Mid- to late April *Gyoki-e,* festival in memory of Honen, the founder of the Jodo sect, several temples.

Late April *Mibu Kyogen,* thirteenth-century dance-dramas, Mibu-ji.

Fourth Sunday in April *Matsuo Matsuri,* portable-shrine parade, Matsuo Taisha.

April–May *Miyako Odori,* cherry-blossom dances, Pontocho Kaburenjo Theater.

Early to mid-May *Kamogawa Odori,* geisha dances, Pontocho Kaburenjo Theater.

Mid-May *Aoi Matsuri,* parade in historical costumes, Kamigamo Shrine and Shimogamo Shrine.

Mid-May *Goryo-e,* procession of palanquins, Shimogamo Shrine.

Third Sunday in May *Mifune Matsuri,* boat festival, Kurumazaki Shrine on the Oi River.

Late May *Shinran Shonin Gotan-e,* festival in memory of Shinran, the founder of the Jodoshin sect, Nishi Hongan-ji.

Early June *Takigi Noh,* evening Noh plays, Heian Shrine.

Late June *Takekiri-e,* ceremonial cutting of bamboo, Kurama-dera.

Mid-July *Gion Matsuri,* procession of decorated floats, Yasaka Shrine.

Late July *Ondasai,* rice-planting festival, Matsuo Taisha.

Mid-August *Daimonji Gozan Okuribi,* hillside fires in the form of Chinese characters, hills outside city.

Mid-August *Toro Nagashi,* lantern festival, Arashiyama Park.

Late August fire festival, banks of river in Hanase.

Late August *Jizo Bon,* children's festival, several temples.

Late August *Nenbutsu Odori,* folk dances, Kisshoin Tenman Shrine.

First Sunday in September *Hassakusai,* harvest festival, Matsuo Shrine.

Early September *Karasu Sumo,* children's sumo wrestling, Kamigamo Shrine.

Late September *Higan-e,* autumnal equinox, all temples.

Early October *Zuiki Matsuri,* procession of decorated floats, Kitano Tenman Shrine.

Early October *Shamenchi Odori,* folk dances, Yase-Akimoto Shrine.

Mid-October *Ushi Matsuri,* traditional costume drama, Koryu-ji.

Late October *Jidai Matsuri,* historical costume parade in commemoration of the founding of the city, Heian Shrine.

Late October *Kurama-no-Himatsuri,* fire festival and torchlight procession, Yuki Shrine.

October–November *Kamogawa Odori,* geisha dances, Pontocho Kaburenjo Theater.

Second Sunday in November *Momiji Matsuri,* tenth-century-style boat trips, Arashiyama Park.

Late November *Ochatsubo Hokensai,* festival commemorating a tea ceremony performed by Toyotomi Hideyoshi in the sixteenth century, Kitano Tenman Shrine.

Late December *Shimai Kobo,* memorial festival for Kobo Daishi, To-ji.

Late December *Tenjin,* festival commemorating Tenjin, Kitano Tenman Shrine.

NARA FESTIVALS

Mid-January *Wakakusayama-yaki,* fireworks and grass burning, Mount Wakakusa.

Early February *Setsubun,* bean-throwing ceremony, Kofuku-ji.

Early February *Onioi-shiki,* exorcism of demons, Kofuku-ji.

Early March *Omizu-tori,* torchlight parade for the drawing of water from a sacred well, Todai-ji.

Early April *Hanae-shiki,* floral offerings for Buddha's birthday, Yakushi-ji.

Early April *Hinae-shiki,* display of thirty images of Zenzaidooji, Hokke-ji.

Second Saturday and Sunday in April *Ocha-mori,* tea ceremony with giant cups, Saidai-ji.

Early May *Shomusai,* traditional procession, Todai-ji.

Mid-May *Takigi Noh,* torchlight Noh plays, Kofuku-ji.

Early June *Kaeru-tobi,* parade of people in frog costumes, Konpusen-ji.

Early August *Daibutsu Ominugui,* ritual cleaning of the Great Buddha, Todai-ji.

Mid-August lantern festival, Kasuga Shrine.

October–November *Shika-no-Tsunokiri,* ceremony to cut the antlers of the deer in Nara Park, Kasuga Shrine.

Mid-November *Kemari Matsuri,* monks play a form of football during the festival, Tanzan Shrine.

Mid-December *Kasuga Wakamiya Matsuri,* parade followed by performances of traditional court music, Kasuga Wakamiya Shrine.

ABOVE: *A procession in traditional court clothing during the Jidai Festival at Heian Shrine.*

(Page 66): *What appears to be a tidal wave of fire during the Omizu-tori festival at Todai-ji in Nara.*

RIGHT: *A cart designed in the style used in the imperial palace hundreds of years ago is decorated with flowers before a procession.*
BELOW: *The casting out of demons at Yakushi-ji.*

ABOVE: *A traditional float in Kyoto's annual Gion Matsuri.*

LEFT: *A procession of Buddhas at Taima-dera.*